DINOSAURS ACTIVITY BOOK

AUTHOR	Charlene Stout
EDITOR	Kathy Rogers
PAGE DESIGN	Linda Milliken
ARTIST	Barb Lorseyedi
COVER DESIGN	Imaginings

METRIC CONVERSION CHART

Refer to this chart when metric conversions are not found within the activity.

¼ tsp	=	1 ml	350° F	=	180° C
½ tsp	=	2 ml	375° F	=	190° C
1 tsp	=	5 ml	400° F	=	200° C
1 Tbsp	=	15 ml	425° F	=	216° C
¼ cup	=	60 ml	1 inch	=	2.54 cm
⅓ cup	=	80 ml	1 foot	=	30 cm
½ cup	=	125 ml	1 yard	=	91 cm
1 cup	=	250 ml	1 mile	=	1.6 km
1 oz.	=	28 g			
1 lb.	=	.45 kg			

©1998 **Edupress, Inc.** • P.O. Box 883 • Dana Point, CA 92629

ISBN 1-56472-126-4
Printed in USA

TABLE OF CONTENTS

LITERATURE LIST

• **Dinosaur Time**
by Peggy Parish;
Harper 1974. (K-2)
Eleven dinosaurs are introduced in this book
for the beginning reader.

• **The Largest Dinosaurs**
by Seymour Simon;
Macmillan 1986. (K-3)
An introduction to the largest of all
dinosaurs—the sauropods.

• **Apatosaurus**
by David Peterson;
Childrens 1989. (1-3)
Formerly known as the Brontosaurus, this
dinosaur is presented in simple, concise text
with color photos.

• **Baby Dinosaurs**
by Helen R. Sattler;
Lathrop 1984. (1-4)
Based on fossil findings, this is a story of how
infant dinosaurs lived.

• **Dinosaur Dig**
by Kathryn Lasky;
Morrow 1990. (1-6)
Chronicles a family's summer experiences in
Montana on a paleontological dig.

• **Dinosaur Hunters**
by Kate McMullan;
Random 1989. (2-4)
An easy reader on how fossils are found and
studied with coverage on new theories about
dinosaurs.

• **The Smallest Dinosaurs**
by Seymour Simon;
Crown paper 1988. (2-4)
An easy-to-read book that gives basic facts and
introduces seven small species.

• **The Last Dinosaur**
by Jim Murphy;
Scholastic 1988. (2-4)
A discussion of why and how the dinosaur
disappeared.

• **Strange Creatures That Really Lived**
by Millicent E. Selsam;
Scholastic 1989. (2-4)
Among the animals featured are giant
dragonflies and flying bats that lived 70 million
years ago.

• **Where Are All the Dinosaurs?**
by Mary O'Neill;
Troll 1989. (2-4)
Author looks at some of the theories regarding
the extinction of the dinosaurs with dinosaur
scenarios and illustrations.

• **Pterosaurs, the Flying Reptiles**
by Helen Sattler;
Lothrop 1985. (2-5)
The pterosaurs are in a class by themselves and
always fascinating to young readers.

• **Dinosaurs All Around: An Artist's
   View of the Prehistoric World**
by Carolyn Arnold;
Houghton 1990. (3-6)
This book concentrates on the art of creating
dinosaur models.

• **Macmillan Children's Guide to Dinosaurs
   and Other Prehistoric Animals**
by Philip Whitfield;
Macmillan 1992. (3-6)
A guide to prehistoric animal life.

• **Your Pet Dinosaur: An Owner's Manual**
by Hudson Talbott;
Morrow 1992. (4-8)
The do's and don't's of having a pet dinosaur.

• **Fossil**
by Paul D. Taylor;
Knopf 1990. (4-8)
This book tells how fossils are formed and what
stories they reveal.

• **Plant-Eating Dinosaurs**
by David Weishampel;
Watts 1992. (4-6)
What did these vegetarians eat and how did
they live for more than 160 million years?

GLOSSARY

amphibian—cold-blooded, frog-like animal that can live partly on land and partly in water, laying its eggs in water.

Archosaurs—dinosaurs descended from this reptile group, including flying, bird-hipped, and lizard-hipped categories.

browsers—animals that feed on the high limbs of shrubs and trees.

carnivore—a meat-eating animal.

carnosaurs—large meat-eating, lizard-hipped dinosaurs with short arms and neck, big head and strong legs.

Ceratopsians—bird-hipped, horned dinosaurs, including Triceratops, Monoclonius, and others.

Coelurosaurids—lizard-hipped, meat-eating dinosaurs with a small head, long neck and slight build.

conifers—trees that bear cones (pine, fir).

continental drift—the process of change in the Earth's surface from the constant motion of the tectonic plates supporting the continents.

cycad—seed-bearing plant that resembles a palm tree.

dinosaurs—prehistoric reptile-hipped and bird-hipped reptiles.

evolution—the slow process by which species change over generations, developing different forms to adapt to new conditions.

forelimb—limb in front (can be an arm, leg, wing, or flipper).

fossil—plant or animal remains buried in the earth and hardened into rock.

ginkgo—a tree in East Asia having yellow flowers and fan-shaped leaves.

Gondwanaland—the ancient southern continent formed when the single land mass, Pangaea, broke in two.

Hadrosaurs—bird-hipped, broad-billed dinosaurs, often with a crest on the head.

herbivore—a plant-eating animal.

horsetail—a fern-like plant having whirls of leaves sprouting from the stem.

invertebrates—animals with no backbone (insects, shellfish).

Laurasia—the ancient northern continent formed when the single land mass, Pangaea, broke in two.

mammal—a warm-blooded, backboned animal that has fur or hair, gives birth to live young, and feeds them milk.

ornithischians—bird-hipped suborder of dinosaurs.

ornithopods—bird-footed dinosaurs.

paleontologist—scientist who studies fossils.

Pangaea—ancient supercontinent that existed when Earth's land masses were joined.

plate tectonics—the study of the movement of the plates of Earth's crust.

Plesiosaurs—turtle-like ocean reptiles having a long snaking neck and paddle-like legs.

Pterosaurs—flying reptiles.

reptiles—cold-blooded, egg-laying, backboned animals.

saurichians—lizard-hipped suborder of dinosaurs.

Sauropods—huge, lizard-hipped, plant-eating dinosaurs with long necks and heavy bodies.

thecodonts—the early ancestors of the dinosaurs.

theropods—meat-eating, lizard-hipped dinosaurs.

vertebrates—animals that have a backbone.

SEDIMENT

INFORMATION

Imagine a scene near a water hole. After a fight-to-the death between *Allosaurus* (al-uh-SORE-us) and *Tyrannosaurus rex* (tie-RAN-uh-SORE-us REX), both dinosaurs fall dead in the mud. Vast oceans ebb and flow, depositing layered depths of *sediment* (sand, mud, and gravel) over them. Volcanoes erupt adding layers of igneous rock on top. The weight of glaciers moving, scraping, and receding gradually turns the surrounding mud into rock as well. Millions of years of earthquakes rattle and raise the fossil bones up within the emerging mountain ranges. Scouring winds and soaking rains gradually wear the stony mud mantle away until a glimpse of bone awaits its discovery by dinosaur hunters or passersby.

Observant travelers can often see different colors in the layers of sediment when they pass a cliff or a deep cut in the earth. The curious stop to examine the layers and feel the earth. Is it hard or soft? Does it crumble easily in your hand? How might the layers have built up over time?

PROJECT

Create a model of sedimentary layers.

MATERIALS

- Small shoe box
- Waxed paper
- Plaster of Paris
- Gray artist's clay
- Bowl
- Mud
- Sand
- Tiny gravel
- Small shells
- Mixing spoon

DIRECTIONS

To prepare sediment layers:

1. Make clay dinosaur bones and allow to dry.

2. Line a shoe box with waxed paper.

3. Mix various elements of sediment with plaster in ½ cup (118 ml) amounts. Place one layer at a time in the box:
   - Plaster and sand with tiny bones
   - Plaster and dirt with larger bones
   - Plaster and gravel
   - Clay imbedded with shells
   - Plaster and sand
   - Plaster and dirt

4. Allow layers of sediment to dry completely at least one day. Peel away the box and waxed paper.

Draw what you observe in each of the following experiments:

- Cut the block into one-inch (2.54 cm) slices to observe what can be seen in the layers.
- Experiment with earthquake uplifting and earth slippage to see how it affects the layers.
- Create a small lake in one piece to observe seepage down through the layers.
- What tiny tools can you use to chip away sediment and clean the bones and shells?

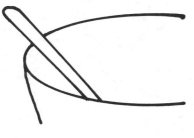

SUPERCONTINENT

INFORMATION

The Earth is not the same as it was 225 million years ago during the Age of the Dinosaurs. At that time the continents were joined together in one supercontinent called *Pangaea* (Pan-JEE-uh). The warm climate allowed the small early dinosaurs to travel widely seeking food.

From 195-136 million years ago, Pangaea separated into two continents—*Laurasia* to the north and *Gondwanaland* to the south. The gigantic plant-eating dinosaurs and the smaller fierce meat-eaters were able to migrate or move long distances by land bridges from one continent to the other.

About 136-165 million years ago, the continents continued to move apart, drifting farther north and south toward the polar regions, settling into today's positions. The repeated climate changes caused the edges of the continents to be flooded. Warm shallow seas spilled over into the low spots of the dry inland deserts bringing moist climates to the areas where dinosaurs ruled.

PROJECT

Move world map pieces backward in time to one big supercontinent.

MATERIALS

• World map, following
• Scissors
• Pencil

DIRECTIONS

1. Make copies of the world map.

2. Cut map into continents. Label them.

3. Move them back together to form one big supercontinent.

WORLD MAP

PALEONTOLOGISTS

INFORMATION

Paleontologists (PAY-lee-un-TOL-uh-jists) are scientists who study living things from the past that are now *extinct,* meaning they have all died out. Searching along muddy lake shores, high rocky cliffs, dry desert hillsides, even leveled construction sites, they discover fossils of extraordinary creatures much like modern reptiles and yet strangely different. Instead of crocodile-like bodies with legs sticking out to the sides, these fossils revealed huge creatures that stood with their feet underneath their bodies. Only recently have paleontologists begun to piece together this Dinosauria puzzle. Each scientist keeps adding more important information to help us understand the unique ancient history of the "Terrible Lizard."

PROJECT

Create simple scripts and present plays of the stories of early paleontologists.

MATERIALS

• Resource books about paleontologists (suggested title: *Dinosaur Hunters* by Kate McMullan)
• Paper
• Pencils
• Props

DIRECTIONS

1. In small groups, allow students to select and do research on a paleontologist or a specific dig.

2. Create short scripts including related bits of information about the dig, tools, bones, difficulties discovering and preserving bones, etc. Encourage creative stage settings and props.

3. Present the plays for another class or as a culminating activity.

FOSSIL HUNT

INFORMATION

Fossils are the traces and remains of once-living creatures (bones, teeth, shells, insects, plants, footprints) found in sedimentary rock—ancient layers of *silt*, sand, and mud. The word fossil means "to dig." Most often that is how people find them. But fossils are not found deep underground. Builders bulldozing in the ground have found them. Others appear on hillsides pushed up by earthquakes, then worn away by wind and water. Fossils have been found by passersby walking along a road or by children playing.

Scientists look for layered sites in the steep sides of a stone quarry, a worn-away hillside, or the cut-away side of a road. Protective clothing and goggles are essential, along with hammers and chisels for carefully breaking up the rock. Paleontologists always draw a map of the site and number each "find" with detailed notes. Fossils and rock samples are kept in bags to be studied extensively back at the lab. Large or extraordinary bones are covered with wet tissues and an open-weave fabric called *scrim*, then covered with plaster of Paris to protect them from damage while being transported. Broken pieces are sometimes temporarily glued together.

PROJECT

Go on a Fossil Hunt for local "finds." Preserve, categorize, and chart what is found.

MATERIALS

- Goggles or sunglasses
- Heavy gloves
- Flat and pointed chisels
- Small hammers
- Hard paint brushes
- Bowl & mixing spoon
- Glue & soft glue brush
- Shoebox
- Tissue paper
- Water
- Plaster of Paris
- Small plastic bags
- Notebook
- Pencil

DIRECTIONS

1. Gather materials and work in small groups.

2. Look for a dig site that contains sedimentary rock and get permission to dig.

3. Chisel away the rock carefully, brushing off dirt with a hard brush.

4. Carefully wrap fossils in tissue paper, coat with plaster of Paris and store in a box.

5. Categorize other objects (rocks, pieces of metal, shells, plant or animal parts, unidentified) in plastic bags.

6. Back in class, chart "finds" as Animal, Mineral or Vegetable, Living or Non-Living, Past or Present, Historical Value or Scrap, etc.

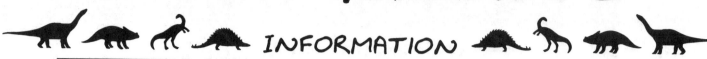

BURIAL GROUNDS

INFORMATION

Fossil bones of dinosaurs have been found on almost every continent of the world, spreading from the equator to the poles. They encompass all the different periods of dinosaur history from the very oldest remains to those existing just before the great extinction. Some regions of the world produced more fossils than others, depending on how much earth uplifting has occurred, as well as wind and weather conditions that have worn away the rock. A considerable variety of dinosaur bones has already been discovered, many in huge piles as if swept together in a giant flood. But many of these ancient giants remain undiscovered, buried in sediment in other great fossil-hunting grounds awaiting new generations of scientists to discover their treasure of fossilized bones.

PROJECT

Locate dinosaur fossil sites on a world map.

DIRECTIONS

1. Use reference books or the chart below to identify world fossil sites.
2. Cut out the dinosaur patterns.
3. Use push pins or tape to attach each dinosaur shape to the area on the world map where its bones were found.

MATERIALS

- Large world map
- Dinosaur patterns, pages 22-24
- Scissors
- Push pins or tape

Allosaurus	Colorado, Utah, Africa, Asia	*Mausasaurus*	Western USA, Kansas
Ankylosaurus	Western North America	*Nodosaurus*	Canada
Archelon	South Dakota	*Ornitholestes*	Central USA
Brachiosaurus	Colorado, Germany, East Africa	*Pachycephalosaurs*	Alberta
		Parasaurolophus	Alberta
Brontosaurus	Europe, Wyoming	*Protoceratops*	Gobi Desert (Mongolia)
Camarasaurus	New Mexico, Montana	*Pteranodon*	Kansas, Texas
Chasmosaurus	Alberta	*Pterodactulus*	Argentina
Corythosaurus	Utah, New Mexico, Canada	*Quetzalcoatlas*	Texas
		Rhamphorhynchus	Germany
Diplodocus	England, Western USA	*Saltopus*	Scotland
Elasmosaurus	Western USA	*Stegosaurus*	Colorado, Wyoming, Utah
Euoplocephalus	Alberta, NW China		
Ichthyosaurus	North & South America, Europe	*Styracosaurus*	Western North America
		Triceratops	Wyoming, Colorado, Canada
Iguanadon	England, Europe, Australia	*Tyrannosaurus Rex*	China, Western USA

BONES

INFORMATION

Bones are the flexible framework of any animal with a backbone. They give it shape, allow it to move, and protects its vital organs. Arm and leg bones are joined together by joints and held together by strong rubber band-like tissue called ligaments. The skull, trunk, and hip bones connect to the spinal column. The neck and back bones are made up of knobby separate bones called vertebrae. Between the vertebrae are round cushioning disks of fibrous cartilage.

Bones are one of the most common animal fossils. The organic material that once filled the microscopic spaces in the bone rot away. Over time the bones are buried in layers of sediment. Water seeping through the ground allows deposits of minerals such as lime or silica to fill in the spaces. The bones become harder and heavier until they appear to become like stone. We say they have become *petrified.*

PROJECT

Examine, identify, compare, and draw or mount bones.

DIRECTIONS

1. Remove as much flesh as possible from the bones.

2. Soak bones ahead of time:

   • Fish bones 15 minutes in soapy water

   • Other bones two hours in soapy water or hydrogen peroxide solution.

3. Examine, identify, and compare the bones, paying particular attention to the neck, hip bones, and joints.

4. Break some extra bones to examine and diagram the inside layers and porous holes.

5. Discuss how these bones might become fossils in time.

6. Draw bones or mount them by gluing together or using heavy wire to stand them up.

MATERIALS

• Bones from turkey, chicken, fish
• Hot soapy water or 10% hydrogen peroxide solution
• Magnifying glass
• Paper
• Pencil
• Cardboard for mounting
• Heavy wire

EARLY PLANTS

The first plants originated in the oceans and moved onto land. They were mostly mosses and ferns. Instead of seeds, they had tiny *spores* which developed into full-sized plants. Needing moist soil, they grew best in swampy areas or near rivers or lakes. As Earth's climate became drier around 300 million years ago, plants with seeds instead of spores developed in the form of palm and pine trees. Plant-eating dinosaurs ate their nutritious leaves and needles.

In some ways dinosaur-age plant life was similar to what we have today—leafy green ferns, low brushy horsetails, palm-like *cycads* on a stocky trunk, club mosses, and conifer trees like our cone-bearing spruce and pine. Flowering plants and grasses did not appear until the end of the dinosaur age.

PROJECT

Research and create a tabletop display of dinosaur-age plants.

MATERIALS

- Reference books
- Borrowed plants
- Index cards
- Pencil

DIRECTIONS

1. Divide class into small groups. Allow each group to choose a plant group to research, find, and borrow for a plant display.

2. Write an information card to identify and describe the plant. Place the card by the plant in the display.

At the beginning of the dinosaur age, living creatures had evolved or slowly changed from single-celled animals into many-celled animals. Gradual adaptations resulted in ancient fish, turtles, two groups of sea reptiles, called *Ichthyosaurs* (IK-thee-uh-sores) and *Plesiosaurs* (PLEH-see-uh-sores), along with frog-like *amphibians* (am-FIB-bee-uns). From snake and lizard-like *Diapsids* (di-AP-sids) came crocodile-like reptiles called *Archosaurs* (ARK-uh-sores.) But instead of legs jutting out from their sides like their elder Archosaurs, the *Thecodants* (THEK-uh-donts) began walking with their legs underneath their bodies. The dinosaurs descended from the Thecodants as either lizard-hipped or bird-hipped creatures. Other Thecodant descendants were crocodiles, flying reptiles called *Pterosaurs* (TAIR-uh-sores), and perhaps even birds.

There were other groups of creatures living in the dinosaur age that evolved differently from the reptiles—shellfish, crab, jellyfish and coral, worms, insects like the cockroach, small shrew-like mammals called *Synapsids (sin-AP-sids),* fish, turtles, and amphibians. These tiny creatures were all food for small meat-eating dinosaurs.

PROJECT

Create an interactive bulletin board of a Dinosaur Family Tree.

MATERIALS

• Brown paper bags
• Stapler
• Blue and green construction paper

DIRECTIONS

1. Twist paper bags or brown craft paper into the shape of tree trunk and limbs. Staple to bulletin board, looping some of the limbs out away from the board to create a three-dimensional tree.

2. Use construction paper to add details to the board: leaves and plants, a lagoon.

3. Use the board for display of dinosaur projects and student work.

DINOSAUR HIPS

INFORMATION

Scientists divide dinosaurs into two main groups of animals according to the way their hip bones were structured. One group was lizard-hipped; the other was bird-hipped. Each group consisted of several different kinds of dinosaurs. They also differed in the way their teeth were made and arranged as well as the size of the holes in their skulls. They had an amazing variety of intelligences, shapes, sizes, speeds, living habits, and temperaments.

The lizard-hipped *Saurischian* (sore-ISS-chee-un) dinosaurs included the giant fearsome meat-eating hunters with saw-teeth and sharp claws. But some of the meat-eaters were no bigger than a large dog. Many of the long-necked, big-bellied giants measuring up to 120 feet (36.6 m) were gentle plant and insect eaters.

The bird-hipped *Ornithischians* (or-nih-THISS-chee-un) appeared after their lizard-hipped kindred. All were plant-eaters with powerful jaws and flat teeth for grinding and chewing plants. They developed unusual body parts—strong muscled legs, flexible necks, horns, spikes, armor-plated skin, bony neck frills, head crests, and tail clubs.

PROJECT

Complete a bar graph that reflects the hip-type group to which each dinosaur belonged.

DIRECTIONS

1. Reproduce the "It's Hip" Dinosaur Graph.

2. Divide into small groups of two or three. Start by placing the dinosaurs in each box into its correct spot on the graph.

3. Continue to research more names and place them correctly in the graph. Extend the length of the graph, if necessary, by gluing additional boxes to the end.

4. Get together to compare information. Combine the names onto one graph. Which hip-type group had the larger dinosaur population?

MATERIALS

- "It's Hip" Dinosaur Graph, following
- Pencil
- Dinosaur resource books

IT'S HIP DINOSAUR GRAPH

Complete the graph to show which hip-type group the different dinosaurs belonged to.

Write each name in its own box on the graph.

Look through more books for "hip" information. Write the dinosaur name in the correct column. Complete as many boxes on the graph as you can.

Use the lists below to get you started.

LIZARD-HIPPED
Brontosaurus
Diplodocus
Brachiosaurus
Allosaurus

BIRD-HIPPED
Ankylosaurus
Stegosaurus
Ornithopods
Ceratopsians

LIZARD-HIPPED   BIRD-HIPPED

IT'S HIP
DINOSAUR GRAPH

Complete the graph to show which hip-type group the different dinosaurs belonged to.

Write each name in its own box on the graph.

Look through more books for "hip" information. Write the dinosaur name in the correct column.
Complete as many boxes on the graph as you can.

Use the lists below to get you started.

LIZARD-HIPPED
Brontosaurus
Diplodocus
Brachiosaurus
Allosaurus

BIRD-HIPPED
Ankylosaurus
Stegosaurus
Ornithopods
Ceratopsians

LIZARD-HIPPED	BIRD-HIPPED

DINOSAUR DIET

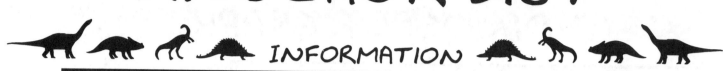

INFORMATION

From the moment they were born dinosaurs had very specialized diets as either meat-eaters, plant-eaters, or egg-eaters. The first thing a mother dinosaur did was to feed her babies. As soon as they were able, plant-eater mothers lead their babies to berry bushes and taught them to feed by example. She took them to streams for water, and later to underbrush to learn to bite off the tough leaves and twigs, and to rake off the pine needles and seeds with their teeth. Meat-eater mothers had a harder job teaching their young to stalk and catch small prey. Even more difficult was the job of the mothers of egg-eaters, who had to teach their youngsters how to steal the eggs of other dinosaurs and carry them away without getting stomped by the angry parents.

PROJECT

Plan, create, and cook food for a dinosaur banquet.

MATERIALS

- Cookbooks
- Utensils, dishes, ingredients for preparation of selected foods

DIRECTIONS

1. Divide the class into three groups: meat-eaters, plant-eaters, and egg-eaters.

2. Using cookbooks, have students brainstorm ideas for recipes and menus that would be appropriate for their dinosaur type.

3. Use the menu-planning guides and recipes to make food assignments, to organize serving and guest table set-up, and to plan decorations.

3. Gather needed food and equipment. Prepare food the day ahead and chill or freeze until time to serve.

BANQUET PLANNING GUIDE

Type of dinosaur attending your banquet (circle one):

Meat-Eater   Plant-Eater   Egg-Eater

Brainstorm a list of foods or recipes appropriate for the dinosaurs attending your banquet:

Final Menu Selection:

Ingredients Needed   Who Will Bring

Equipment Needed   Who Will Bring

TEETH

A quick look at a dinosaur's teeth will tell you if it was a meat-eater or a plant-eater. Meat-eaters' teeth were sharp, saw-toothed or dagger-like, sometimes pointing backwards for hooking, gripping, or tearing flesh from their victims. Most plant-eaters had hundreds of flat, chisel-like teeth for chopping and grinding up tough plant material. *Diplodocus* (dih-PLOD-uh-cus) had thin, pencil-like teeth at the front of its mouth for raking along branches to draw in fern and palm leaves, pine needles, and pine cone seeds. With no back teeth for chewing, Diplodocus just swallowed. During their entire life, both meat-eaters and plant-eaters constantly grew new teeth to replace old, worn, and lost teeth.

PROJECT

Examine your own teeth to determine if you are a meat-eater or a plant-eater.

MATERIALS

• Hand mirror

DIRECTIONS

1. Using a mirror, study your front teeth first. Are they pencil-like for raking, sharp and pointed for tearing, or flat and chisel-like for grinding?

2. Study your back teeth next. Are they flat like chisels, pointy, or pencil-like?

3. What conclusions can you come to? Are you a meat-eater or a plant-eater?

4. Will your teeth constantly replace themselves your whole life?

5. Discuss and demonstrate what people do to care for their teeth.

EGGS AND BABIES

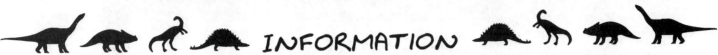

Female dinosaurs laid their eggs in nests dug in the ground, often in a bowl-like mound covered with sand or leaves. The mothers were too heavy to sit on the eggs the way a chicken does. The sun warmed the eggs and helped them to hatch. When it was time, the eggs began to move. Some tiny dinosaurs had a special tooth for pecking at the eggshells until their little heads and bodies could pop out. That tooth would soon fall out after the dinosaur was hatched. When they stumbled out of their shells, the hatchlings found themselves in a field packed full of circular nests, new babies and mothers nearby.

Some dinosaur mothers left newly-hatched babies to fend for themselves. Some even ate their own babies. But other mothers brought their babies food, stayed by the nest, and taught them where to find berries and water. When it was time to leave the nests, the herd traveled with the young in the middle for protection from enemies. To survive, the dinosaur offspring had to learn how to eat tough leaves, bark, twigs, bushes, and water plants, or to hunt for their own meat. All the while they had to keep a sharp watch out for the meat-eaters looking for their next meal.

Many of these dinosaur nests containing fossilized eggs have been found in the last 50 years—some with tiny fossil bones still inside the eggs and the mothers' bodies nearby.

PROJECT

Make a baby dinosaur hatching from its egg. Write a documentary from the perspective of the newly-hatched dinosaur.

DIRECTIONS

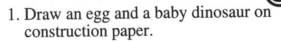

1. Draw an egg and a baby dinosaur on construction paper.

2. Color and cut them out.

3. Cut the egg in half using a zig-zag cutting line to represent a broken eggshell.

4. Use a brad to connect the two pieces of eggshell with the dinosaur behind it (see illustration).

MATERIALS

- Construction paper
- Colored markers
- Scissors
- Brad
- Pencil

LITTLE EGG THIEF

INFORMATION

The "little egg-thief" was *Oviraptor* (O-vuh RAP-tor), a small dinosaur with a big taste for eggs. Only three feet (1 m) long, this hungry hunter had no teeth so meat-eating was a problem. Sucking eggs and munching the soft-boned, newly hatched baby dinosaurs was the solution. If he could not find eggs, fruits and other soft foods would do.

Many dinosaurs laid their eggs on top of the ground, left to hatch unguarded. Some scientists believe increasing numbers of Oviraptors and small mammals may have eaten too many eggs. With fewer dinosaurs being born, they would quickly become extinct.

Paleontologists have found nests of Protoceratops eggs with the small thief, the mother, and the eggs buried together when a great sandstorm came whirling in, covering all in many feet of sand. Over time the sand weighed down and cracked the egg shells. The runny liquid seeped out. Sand sifted in, filling the space. Pressure over millions of years changed the eggs to rock, frozen in time for eons.

PROJECT

Experiment to find out what foods an Oviraptor might have eaten.

DIRECTIONS

1. As a class, discuss what types of foods might be eaten without chewing.

2. Assign students to bring in food samples. Cut into small pieces.

3. Sample the different foods, trying not to use teeth.

4. Draw conclusions about what kind of diet an Oviraptor might have had.

MATERIALS

- Foods as needed (see directions)
- Kitchen knives, cutting boards, serving plates

DINOSAUR COLORS

INFORMATION

Paleontologists have found extensive digs of bones to reconstruct the skeletons of dinosaurs of all shapes. They range in size from as tiny as a chicken to six stories tall. The remarkable diversity of shapes runs from sleek to absolutely strange. But there is little real scientific evidence to tell us the type or color of the dinosaurs' skin covering. Just as today's animals are designed for survival and for blending in with their surroundings, so the gentle plant-eaters must have had nature's camouflage colors to enable them to rest safely in a shady grove hidden from the savage meat-eaters. Large neck frills may have been brightly colored to frighten off an enemy, to attract a mate, or to signal their own kind. Only illustrations of *Archaeopteryx* (ar-kee-OP-ter-ix) use bold bright colors. Is it possible the gangly flying Pterosaurs (TAIR-uh-sores) may have been beautiful as well?

PROJECT

Do research to hypothesize and draw conclusions about the color of dinosaurs' skin.

DIRECTIONS

1. Work in pairs to choose a dinosaur from the fact-finding cards. Select the corresponding dinosaur pattern.

2. Do research to learn about the environment of the selected dinosaur. After discussion, make hypotheses about how the dinosaurs' skin might have been adapted for its surroundings.

3. Use a transparency and projector to enlarge a front and back pattern onto paper and cut out.

4. Staple the front and back together, leaving an opening for stuffing. Use markers to decorate the dinosaur. Stuff with tissue or shredded newspaper. Staple opening closed.

5. Place dinosaurs on the interactive dinosaur tree (page 13) in an appropriate spot. Suspend the flying creatures from the ceiling with fishing line.

MATERIALS

• Transparency film and projector
• Paper
• Fishing line
• Dinosaur patterns, pages 22-24
• Dinosaur fact cards, pages 40-42
• Reference books
• Colored marking pens
• Tissue or shredded newspaper
• Pencils

DINOSAUR PATTERNS

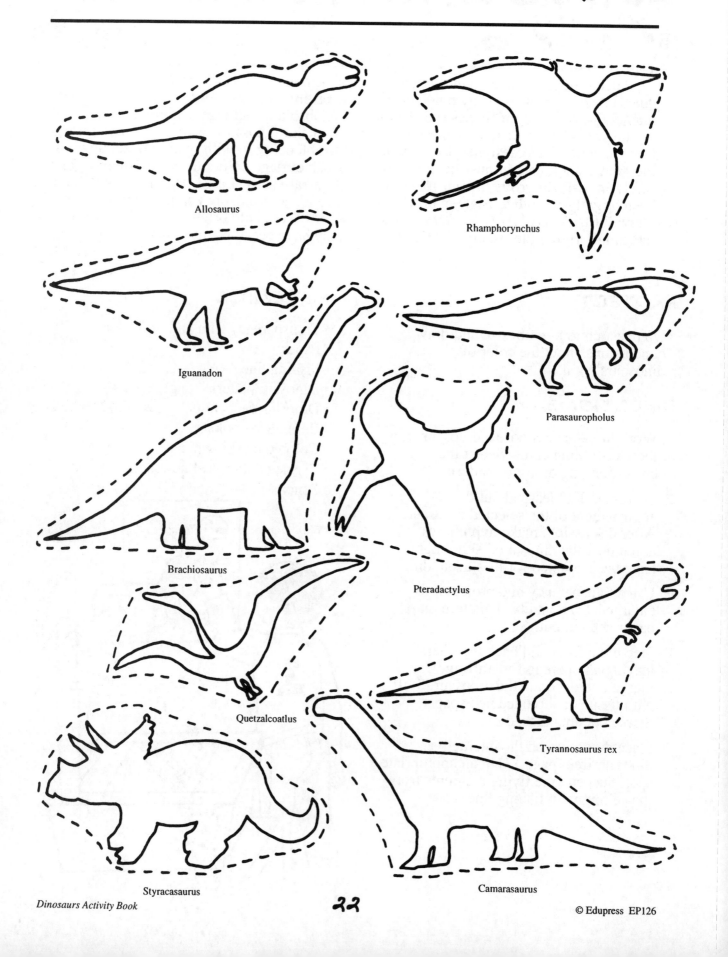

Allosaurus

Rhamphorynchus

Iguanadon

Parasauropholus

Brachiosaurus

Pteradactylus

Quetzalcoatlus

Tyrannosaurus rex

Styracasaurus

Camarasaurus

Ichthyosaurus

Protocertatops

Chasmosaurus

Maiasaura

Dimetrodon

Pachycephalosaurus

Pteranodon

Brontosaurus

Saltopus

Corythosaurus

Nodasaurus

Ankylosaurus

Euoplocephalus

Triceratops

Diplodocus

Ornitholestes

Archaeopteryx

Archelon

Elasmosaurus

Stegosaurus

EARLY SAIL-SPINES

INFORMATION

Lizards of today bask in the early morning sunshine warming their blood to get the jump on still-cold, sluggish prey. *Dimetrodon* (die-ME-tro-don) was an early sail-spined dinosaur who did just that millions of years ago. This large 11-foot (3-m) meat-eating lizard had a spectacular sail-like fin full of small blood vessels on its back. Scientists believe the sail regulated its body temperature. Dimetrodon could simply turn its sail broadside toward the sun to soak up the rays of heat and transmit the warmth throughout its body. For cooling down it merely turned to face the afternoon sun head-on.

PROJECT

Conduct thermometer experiments to determine what other physical properties may have been present in the sail to help soak up the sun's heat.

DIRECTIONS

1. Divide the class into small groups to brainstorm other factors that may have contributed to the sail's ability to soak up the sun's heat.

2. Have students list ideas regarding size, density, type, and color of various materials to test.

3. Have students collect materials on their list.

4. Using the Dimetrodon sail pattern, have them cut a variety of sails out of each material. Lay each one over a thermometer and place them in full sun. Record temperatures for each material. Which had the best heat retention?

5. When the experiment is completed, stand the Dimetrodon sails on end, facing head-on into the sun. Retest three of the best heat-retaining materials to see how much cooler this position would have been. Write up the experiment and its results and post it on the dinosaur board.

MATERIALS

- Small thermometers
- Cardboard for Dimetrodon sail pattern, below
- Window with full sun
- Paper
- Pencil
- Scissors
- Variety of materials (students supply such materials as thin parchment, thin sheet of sponge, light and dark construction paper, aluminum foil, paper towels, clear plastic wrap, wax paper, etc.)

ARCHAEOPTERYX

INFORMATION

When is a bird not a bird? Some scientists would answer, "When it is called Archaeopteryx." Living 150 million years ago, it had wings and feathers and it could fly, although not as well as today's birds. However, many scientists believe Archaeopteryx is merely the missing link between birds and dinosaurs. If so, then who do they say is the first bird?

Archaeopteryx's skeleton is almost identical to that of the chicken-sized dinosaur, *Compsognathus* (COM-sog-NATH-us), except for the longer hands, bird hips, and feathers. Other scientists point to a dinosaur named *Protoavis* (Pro-toe-AV-iss) which means "First Bird." Appearing 75 million years before Archaeopteryx, it had time to evolve into the first gulls and herons.

PROJECT

Create an Archaeopteryx hanging.

DIRECTIONS

1. Copy the Archaeopteryx pattern. Design a bird-like head.

2. Boldly color the feathers and cut the bird-shape out.

3. Create a cross-shaped cardboard frame for the backside of Archaeopteryx and glue it on.

4. Attach string or fishing line to suspend the Archaeopteryx from the ceiling or from the overhanging branches of the interactive dinosaur tree (page 13).

MATERIALS

- Archaeopteryx pattern, following
- Paper
- Cardboard strips for framework
- Bold colored marking pens
- Scissors
- Glue
- String or fishing line

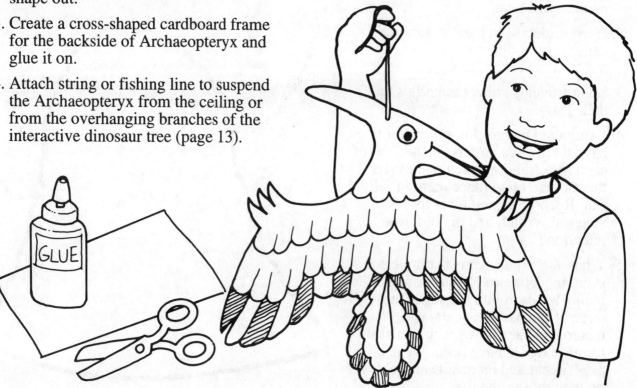

ARCHAEOPTERYX

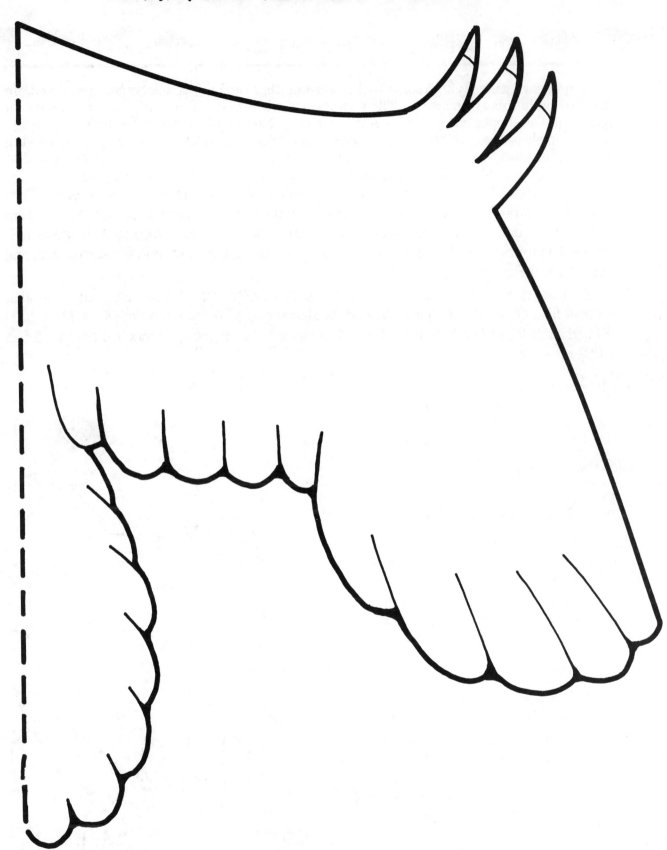

PTEROSAURS

INFORMATION

Pterosaurs were flying reptiles who were neither bird nor dinosaur but evolved from similar evolutionary ancestors. Their enormous wings were simply a large membrane of skin that was supported by an elongated "pinky" finger and attached at the bottom to weak, almost useless legs which made walking very awkward. Three other fingers mid-wing were small with hook-like claws. Because flight was so demanding, they are believed to have been warm-blooded and may have been covered with fur instead of feathers.

Pterosaurs had large heads with long jaws full of sharp teeth that slanted forward. They ate fish, soft-bodied insects, and the dead remains of other animals. Their bones were hollow but very strong. Babies emerged from their eggs not completely formed, their wings developing after hatching. Some Pterosaurs had a pouch of skin for storing fish and insects for their babies.

Pterosaurs were divided into two categories: (1) Pterosaurs had very long thin tails, some with a spear-like rudder at the end for steering. (2) *Pterodactyls (TAIR-uh-DAK-tulz)* all had short tails or no tails at all. Some were as small as pigeons, others had bodies 15 feet (4.57 m) long.

PROJECT

Play an outdoor game of "Pterosaurs Fly!"

DIRECTIONS

1. Divide the class into two teams, one the Pterosaurs, the other the Pterodactyls.

2. Line teams up at the opposite ends of a lined grassy playing field. The teacher or a student is the caller.

3. The teams come to the center of the field. If the caller yells out "Pterosaurs chase!" the Pterosaurs try to *tag* the players on the other team before they reach the safety of their cliffs (their back line.).

4. If the caller yells "Pterodactyls chase!" the Pterodactyl team tries to *tag* the other team.

5. Players who are tagged are taken as prisoners and remain at the enemies' cliffs until each round is over.

6. After ten rounds the team with the most captives wins and play begins anew.

SEA REPTILES

INFORMATION

Fossils buried in long-gone sea beds reveal an interesting assortment of sea creatures, some much like we see today. *Archelon* (AR-kee-lon), the "ruler turtle," did not have a hard shell but rather a lighter body framework. Huge prehistoric crocodiles would lay like dead logs waiting for unsuspecting plant-eaters.

But others were truly giant sea monsters. *Plesiosaurus* (PLEH-see-uh-SORE--us) had a large saucer-shaped body with a tiny head atop an extended snake-like neck and a long rudder-tipped tail, looking very much like Scotland's mysterious Loch Ness creature. Air-breathing *Icthyosaurus* (IK-thee-uh-SORE-us) was shaped more like our modern dolphins and varied greatly in size. These powerful swimmers slashed through a school of fish until the school moved on and then leisurely ate the victims. *Mausasaurus* (MO-zuh-SORE-us) were reptiles with frog-like webbed feet, a long flat eel-like tail, and crocodile-like thin jaws with daggers for teeth.

PROJECT

Model some of the prehistoric sea reptiles in clay and display with identifying cards.

DIRECTIONS

1. Research a prehistoric sea reptile.

2. Working on plastic or aluminum, work the clay with your hands until it is the consistency of cream cheese.

3. Keep models small and "close to the ground" for stability. Starting with a ball for the body, mold, pull out, pinch off, and stick on until you get the body just right. Use bent nails to support legs or splay them out to the sides. Decide whether the sea reptile will have smooth or bumpy skin. Dry completely before painting.

4. Mount with glue to a board base. Write an identifying label with a brief description on an index card and attach it to the model.

MATERIALS

- Fact Cards, pages 22-24
- Air-drying modeling or potter's clay
- Spray-bottle of water
- Plastic knives, forks, and spoons for tools
- Plastic or aluminum worksheets
- Small boards for mounting
- Bent nails for leg support
- Plastic bags to store leftover clay
- Glue
- Index cards
- Pencils

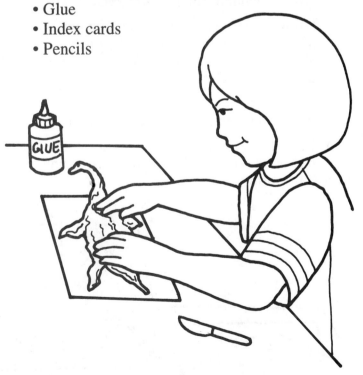

SMALL NEIGHBORS

INFORMATION

Dinosaurs were not the only animals living millions of years ago. Other animals shared the landscape with them. Lizards, turtles, crocodiles, and snakes all looked much the same as they look today. Fish appeared 500 million years ago, long before the dinosaurs. The oceans were filled with dolphin-like *Ichthyosaurs* (IK-thee-uh-sores) and paddle-flippered *Plesiosaurs* (PLEH-see-uh-sores), primitive jellyfish, shellfish, and coral. Early amphibians like newts and frogs existed both in water and on land. The enormous *Mastodonsaurus* (MASS-tuh-don-SORE-us) was a frog-like crocodile with a 4½-foot (1.37 m) skull. It fed on dragonflies with 30-inch (81-cm) wings. Foot-long (30-cm) cockroaches looked like our modern smaller version. Two-thirds of the insects existing in the world today existed alongside the dinosaurs. The world's first mammals were small creatures called *synapsids* (sin-AP-sids) that looked much like shrews and mice of today.

PROJECT

Create a dinosaur scene of family groups in their appropriate setting with their "small neighbors" and plants.

DIRECTIONS

1. Use colored paper to line the box to represent landscape and surroundings—sky, water, sandy shore, mountains, grassy lowlands, plants, and trees.

2. Using construction paper, cut silhouettes of the dinosaurs in your family group, along with some of the small neighbors listed above. Glue to appropriate spots in the scene.

3. Add rocks, twigs, and redwood chips.

4. Cut a 1 x 2-inch (2.54 x 5-cm) slit in the lid and in one side of box for viewing and for lighting.

MATERIALS

• Large box with removable lid
• Colored paper
• White paper
• Dark-colored construction paper
• Glue
• Rocks, twigs, redwood chips
• Scissors

SAUROPODS

The *sauropods* (SORE-uh-pods) were the long-necked plant-eaters, the largest of all land animals. The silted floodplain on the eastern side of the Rocky Mountains between New Mexico and Montana was the home of large herds of sauropods, including Diplodocus, *Apatosaurus* (uh-PAT-uh-SORE-us)—also called *Brontosaurus* (BRON-tuh-SORE-us)—*Camarasaurus* (CAM-are-uh-SORE-us), and *Brachiosaurus* (BRACH-ee-uh-SORE-us). Much of the sauropods' length came from their extraordinarily long necks and tails. Many early scientists insisted the long necks indicated that the huge bodies of these creatures were underwater most of the time to support their tremendous weight. It is now believed the long necks were for nibbling leaves from the tops of trees. Scientists find larger and larger sauropods, with *Ultrasaurus* (UL-truh-SORE-us) measuring 100 feet (30.48 m) long and 150 tons (.90 metric tons) and *Seismosaurus* (SIZE-muh-SORE-us) at 120 feet (36.58 m)!

The teeth of most plant-eaters were flat, chisel-like, and arranged all along the jaws. Others like Diplodocus had teeth bunched at the front of the mouth for raking leaves and needles from branches. Piles of polished stones indicate they probably swallowed stones to help grind up the food in their stomachs, much as chickens do.

PROJECT

Conduct an experiment to observe what happens in a plant-eater's stomach.

DIRECTIONS

1. Divide the class into three groups.

2. Put an equal amount of leaves, large seeds, pine needles and pine cones in each of the plastic bags.

3. In the first bag add only large stones, in the second only small stones and in the third an equal mixture of both large and small stones. Press the air out of the bags and zip closed to seal.

4. Group members take turns kneading the bags to grind up the material inside for a set amount of time.

5. Compare and discuss the results. Which size stones would have best ground up the leaves and seeds eaten by the plant-eating dinosaurs?

MATERIALS

- Three zip-lock plastic bags
- Large and small stones
- Leaves
- Large seeds
- Pine needles and cones
- Pencil
- Paper

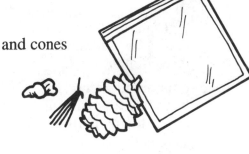

BRONTOSAURUS

INFORMATION

The "thunder lizard" Brontosaurus, often called Apatosaurus, was the big-footed gentle giant of the cruel world of dinosaurs. His flat, spoon-shaped teeth, perfect for snipping and eating water plants, would have been little defense against fierce meat-eaters. But this slow-witted, blimp-bodied animal, 29 feet (8.8 m) tall at the shoulders, 70 feet (21.3 m) long, and weighing 36 tons (32.7 metric tons), could look intimidating stomping along, shaking the ground with a sound like thunder. Living by the marshy edges of prehistoric lakes in Wyoming, these trunk-legged creatures left thousands of perfect imprints of their padded elephant-like feet that measured over 2½ feet (.76 m) in diameter. Just imagine a footprint the size of a bass drum!

Fossil footprints are important as clues not only to the size of the dinosaur's feet, but also how heavy it was, how and where it walked, how it moved, how fast it traveled, and if it could swim. Dinosaur parks have been developed so people can see and walk in the fossilized tracks of these ancient creatures.

PROJECT

Research and make cast fossils of Brontosaurus and other dinosaurs' footprints.

DIRECTIONS

1. Research and draw on cardboard various dinosaur footprints, labeling each by name. Try adding layers to make them three-dimensional.

2. Pour about ½ cup (125 ml) of plaster of Paris into a bowl. Add water a little at a time, stirring until it is the consistency of cake batter.

3. Gently and carefully press the "fossil" footprint into the wet plaster and allow it to dry.

4. Remove the cardboard and observe the fossil imprint.

5. Use an index card to label and describe your dinosaur and the imaginary site where the footprint was found.

Remind students *never* to pour the left-over plaster down a sink drain!

MATERIALS

- Fact Cards, pages 40-42
- Reference books
- Plaster of Paris or artist's clay
- Corrugated cardboard
- Water
- Paper soup bowls
- Plastic spoons for stirring
- Index cards
- Pencils

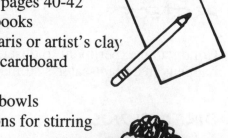

BRACHIOSAURUS

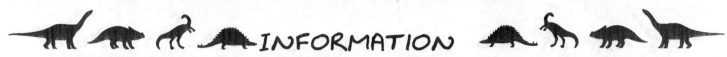

INFORMATION

Brachiosaurus was the tallest dinosaur, measuring 40 feet (12 m) at its shoulders. Though not as long as Diplodocus or Brontosaurus, it was the heaviest land animal that ever lived. This giant plant-eater was 80 feet (24 m) long and weighed over 70 tons (63.5 metric tons). It consumed five tons (4.5 metric tons) of plants each day! Because its front legs were longer than the back legs it could reach branches as high as a three-story building. The huge-bellied, long-necked, small-headed, tiny-brained dinosaurs were probably not very smart. But they knew their best escape from the fierce meat-eaters was to wade deeper into a lake until only their nose holes protruded above the water.

PROJECT

Conduct a fun food-weight comparison to determine how many sack lunches Brachiosaurus would have eaten daily to meet his five-ton (4.5 metric tons) quota.

DIRECTIONS

1. Instruct students to bring a sack lunch for the comparison.

2. Weigh the amount of food in each student's sack before they go to lunch. Figure the total weight and average per sack lunch.

3. Ask students to use lunch time to figure how many sack lunches it would take to weigh five tons (4.5 metric tons).

4. Write up and post the comparison as well as the names of students who came up with the correct answer.

MATERIALS

- Sack lunch from each student
- Paper
- Pencils
- Food scale measuring in pounds and ounces (kg and g)

DIPLODOCUS

INFORMATION

Diplodocus (dih-PLOD-uh-cus) was a plant-eating dinosaur that measured longer than three big city buses! It stood 13 feet (4 m) high at the shoulders, was about 80 feet (24 m) long, and weighed 20 tons (18.2 metric tons). It was considerably lighter than Brontosaurus because its more slender body was mostly long, thin, and snaky at both ends. Its strong back muscles led down into a powerful thick tail that narrowed to a whip-like end used for defense. Like many of the other large dinosaurs, Diplodocus was probably not very smart. Their best defense was to seek safety in deep water. The short stubby pencil-like teeth located at the front of their mouth indicate they bit off soft water-plants that grew along the shore, and they may have swallowed their food whole.

PROJECT

Measure a school bus to demonstrate the massive length of Diplodocus.

MATERIALS

• Ball of heavy string
• Paper
• Pencil
• School bus

DIRECTIONS

1. Using sturdy string, measure the length of one bus.

2. On the playground, use the string to lay out and measure the length of three school buses.

3. Have students lay end to end to show how long Diplodocus was.

4. Encourage them to create math problems to explain what they have shown.

5. Have students write up their experience as a short story for the classroom or school newsletter.

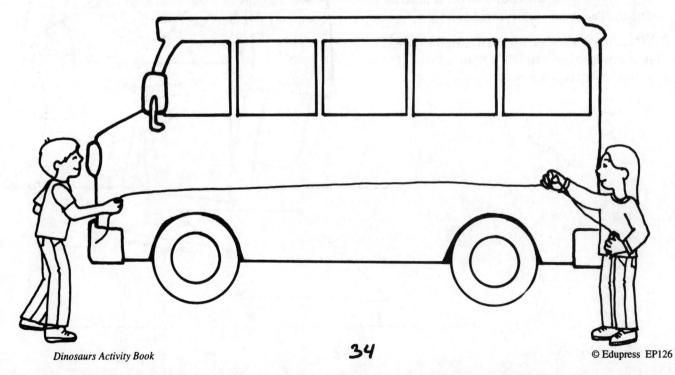

CARNOSAURS

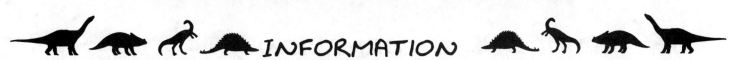

Carnosaurs were the large meat-eating hunters of the ancient world. While the sauropod herbivores (plant-eaters) came in a wide variety of kinds, sizes, and shapes, the two-legged carnosaurs all developed the same basic body type. Their powerful hind legs allowed them to move quickly while their muscular tail balanced their upright stance. Their tiny weak forearms probably were used to tear apart their prey after the kill and help them to rise from their resting place. Small hands had two or three fingers, each with a sharp claw. Their large skulls held powerful jaws lined with dagger-like teeth designed for slashing flesh. The smaller versions depended on their ostrich-like legs, good eyesight and fierce nature to make them adept at stalking and killing much larger animals. Hunting in herds, they ran fast and upright on long slender hind legs. Their speed was used both to catch their prey and to escape their predators.

PROJECT

Create aclass flip book about Carnosaurs.

DIRECTIONS

1. Divide the construction paper into 3 x 6-inch (7.6 x 15.2-cm) sections with broken lines to indicate five cutting lines and a heavy solid center fold line as shown below.

2. Draw a picture of a dinosaur that is a carnosaur sized to fit on one of the top flaps.

3. On a piece of writing paper, write a description containing a minimum of four interesting facts about the dinosaur.

4. Glue the picture on the top flap and the description directly under it on the lower flap.

MATERIALS

- Construction paper, 12 x 18 inches (30.5 x 45.7 cm)
- Colored marking pens
- Scissors
- Writing paper cut in 3 x 6-inch (7.6 x 15.2-cm) pieces
- Pencil
- Glue

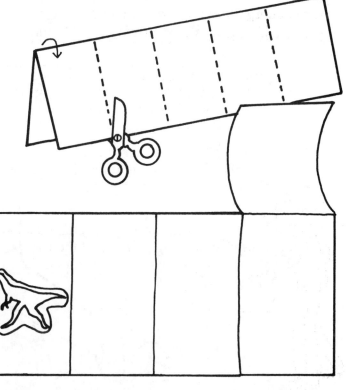

TYRANNOSAURUS REX

INFORMATION

The fierce and fearsome Tyrannosaurus rex (tie-RAN-uh-SORE-us REX), the "tyrant lizard king," was the largest meat-eating land animal. Weighing 6 tons (54.4 metric tons) and standing as high as a large giraffe, this 50-foot (15-m) long meat-eater had a massive head with huge jaws lined with sixty teeth, including the largest of all the dinosaur teeth ever discovered. Its teeth were six inches (15.2 cm) long, sharp, and blade-like, with serrated edges for stabbing and tearing meat. Walking quickly on two massive hind legs, huge tail swishing behind, and clawed feet sinking deep in the mud, it would stalk even the largest creatures. Some scientists believe Tyrannosaurus spent much of the time resting and feeding on the carcasses killed by other dinosaurs too intimidated to hold on to their prey. Tyrannosaurus' skinny little arms and tiny two-fingered hands were probably useful merely for helping it to rise from the ground.

PROJECT

Conduct a "strait-jacket" experiment to find uses for Tyrannosaurus's arms and two-fingered hands.

MATERIALS

• Heavy masking tape
• Paper
• Pencil

DIRECTIONS

1. Divide the class into small groups. Each group selects one person to be Tyrannosaurus.

2. Gently tie the arms of the Tyrannosaurus pretender to their body. Tape the thumbs and all but two fingers down gently to the hands.

3. Each group brainstorms a list of activities to attempt (eating, writing, reading, lying down and rising up, drinking from a stream, etc.).

4. Have groups report back any possible uses they discovered for the tiny arms and hands, as well as all the things they couldn't do.

5. Allow two "Tyrannosaurus" to pretend to have a slow-motion fight. Without the use of hands and arms, what other "weapons" might they have used?

ALLOSAURUS

INFORMATION

Allosaurus has been called a dinosaur's worst nightmare. Also called *Antrodemus* (an-tro-DEE-mus), this vicious meat-eater was 36 feet (11 m) from tip of nose to tip of tail. It had a massive 3-foot (1-m) skull with great gaping, hinged jaws full of three-inch (7.6 cm) daggers for teeth. Using its powerful bird-like, clawed hind legs and strong tail for balance, it was able to run at high speeds in pursuit of the largest creatures of its day. Its strong front legs were too short to support the weight of its two-ton (1.8 metric tons) body, but three large claws made them useful for slashing and gripping in an attack. It is believed that Allosaurus hunted in packs. They hid and spied from the cover of forests, crashing quickly into the open marshland to attack from the rear, finishing off their victims in seconds, then feeding on the kill for many days.

PROJECT

Create a display of authentic-looking clay teeth for Allosaurus and Tyrannosaurus.

DIRECTIONS

1. Select the pattern for the Allosaurus or Tyrannosaurus tooth.

2. Using clay, sculpt a tooth to authentic size.

3. On an index card, write the name and a brief description of the tooth.

Extended Activity:

Create an authentic dinosaur jaw. How many teeth would go in it? What would the teeth look like? Again, use index cards to label and describe the creations.

MATERIALS

• Cardboard teeth patterns below
• Clay
• Index cards
• Pencils

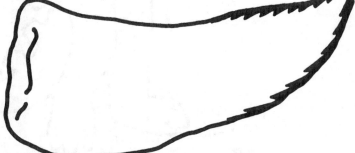

DINO DEFENSES

INFORMATION

Fossils reveal the many ways the often small-brained, slow-witted dinosaurs defended themselves. The plant-eaters' teeth and feet indicate they probably didn't attack other animals, but they developed a wide variety of other weapons and defenses. Some used their thrashing muscular tails, their massive body weight, and their heavy elephant-sized feet to crush their attackers. Other dinosaurs developed bony heads, impenetrable neck shields, armored body plates, long horns, sharp spikes and claws, even heavy clubs at the ends of their tails—all in an attempt to ward off the ever-attacking meat-eaters. Many dinosaur families traveled in herds with the young and the weak in the center. The duck-billed and the blimp-bellied, long-necked plant-eaters' best defense was the most simple. They completely submerged themselves for long periods in deep water. Only their tiny nose openings on the very top of their skulls appeared out of the water.

PROJECT

Create a costume that reflects how the dinosaur body was adapted for defense.

DIRECTIONS

1. Divide into cooperative groups of three to four studemts.

2. Discuss the unusual body features some dinosaurs had that provided them with a means of defense. Refer to pages 40-42 for this information.

3. Each group selects a dinosaur and creates a costume that shows that dinosaur's body adaptation. Be imaginative in the use of materials. Embellish with hats, belts, fabric, paper bags, and other student-supplied materials.

4. Ask one student in the group to don the costume while the rest of the group presents a short explanation. A mock "battle of the dinosaurs" may follow the presentations! (See page 39.)

MATERIALS

• Poster board
• Scissors
• Marking pens
• Colored paper
• Tempera paints and brushes
• Assorted art materials
• Student-supplied costume materials

DINO DEFENSES

PROJECT

Write and present a radio broadcast.

MATERIALS

- Large sheet
- Clothesline
- Instruments and objects for sound effects

DIRECTIONS

1. Suspend the clothesline across a section of the classroom. Hang the sheet over the clothesline to create a curtain.

2. Work in the same cooperative groups as formed for the costume creation on the preceding page.

3. Imagine two dinosaurs in battle and write a script for a radio broadcast that presents a blow-by-blow description of the battle. Use descriptive phrases and voice inflection to add to the drama.

4. Create sound effects to accompany the script.

5. Present the radio broadcast from behind the curtain.

DINOSAUR FACT CARDS

Allosaurus
(al-uh-SORE-us)
"delicate strange lizard"

• 36 feet (11 m) long • Weighed 2 tons (1.8 metric tons) • Used thick heavy tail to balance while running upright on strong speedy legs • 3 toes with sharp talons • 3 fingers with 6-inch (15-cm) claws • Short, strong neck • Head 3 feet (.9 m) long • Powerful hinged jaws, 4-inch (10-cm) dagger-like teeth • Hunted large dinosaurs in packs

Ankylosaurus
(an-KILE-uh-SORE-us)
"curved lizard"

• Peaceful plant-eating "army tank" • Husky 4-foot (1.2-m) high body • 25 feet (7.6 m) long and weighed 5 tons (4.5 metric tons) • Armor of thick bony plates, nodules, and rows of short spikes covering leathery skin • Ridged crest in middle for strength • Short, thick tail ended in bony club to swing at enemy • Beak-like mouth, massive jaws, weak teeth

Archelon
(AR-kee-lon)
"ruler turtle"

Large heavy sea turtle • Grew up to 12 feet (3.7 m) long • Lived in an inland sea • Body covering was not a hard solid turtle shell but just a framework of bones • Flipper-like front legs effective in water but not strong enough to get to beach • Swam in with rising tide to lay its eggs in the sand, then rode the next high tide out

Brachiosaurus
BRACK-ee-uh-SORE-us)
"arm lizard"

• Lived on lake edges, forests of river plains • Ate 5 tons (4.5 metric tons) of plants daily • 40 feet (12 m) tall, 80 feet (24 m) long • Weighed 70 tons (63.5 metric tons) • Could swim • Trunk-like legs, huge padded feet • Towering 30-foot (9-m) neck • Small head with nasal holes at top • High shoulders, long forearms gave a downward slope to the back

Brontosaurus
(BRON-tuh-SORE-us)
"thunder lizard"

• Also called *Apatosaurus* • Large as two schoolrooms • 70 feet (21.3 m) long, 29 feet (8.8 m) tall • Weighed over 36 tons (32.7 metric tons) • Rear legs longer than the front legs • Feet like an elephant's • Neck longer than its body • Tiny head with fist-sized brain • Small peg-like teeth • Tough leathery skin • Size offered protection

Camarasaurus
(CAM-are-uh-SORE-us)
"chambered lizard"

• Small husky body with short neck and tail • 50 feet (15.2 m) in length • Horizontal back did not slope • Large box-like skull, full of holes • Huge nostrils high on its head to cool the brain in hot weather • Long jaws filled with strong, chisel-like teeth for eating tougher plants • Spongy wedge of tissue beneath heel to help bear the great body weight

Chasmosaurus
(KAZ-mo-SORE-us)
"cleft lizard"

• First of the long-frilled dinosaurs • Large heart-shaped frill extended sail-like over shoulders and forearms • 17 feet (5.2 m) long • Weighed 4 tons (3.6 metric tons) • Perhaps brightly colored to attract attention • Long eyebrow horns, short nose horn • Beaked nose to bite off plants • Herd frightened enemies by facing outward to form a wall of frills

Corythosaurus
(cu-RIE-thu-SORE-us)
"helmet lizard"

• Bony helmet-shaped head • When threatened they went into the water, swam deeper and deeper until they needed to surface for air, filled their hollow skulls with air, and returned to feed on the bottom until the danger passed • 35 feet (10.7 m) long • Plant-eaters • Nested together in flamingo-like nests • Cared for their young

Diplodocus
(dih-PLOD-uh-cus)
"double beam"

• Longer than 3 buses • 90 feet (27.4 m) long, 13 feet (4 m) high • Weighed 20 tons (18 metric tons) • Small head for a giant body • Elephant-like legs and feet • Powerful back muscles • Strong thick tail for balance, ended in whiplash for defense • Incisor-like teeth bunched at the front of its jaws for snipping but not for chewing

Elasmosaurus
(ee-LAZ-muh-SORE-us)
"thin-plated lizard"

• Largest of the plesiosaurs • True sea-monster with a short, rounded body • 60 feet (18 m) long • Looked like a snake drawn through a turtle-like body • 4 powerful paddle-like flippers • Slow-moving creature that lived at the surface of the ocean • Jaws filled with sharp teeth perfect for catching and eating fish and diving birds

DINOSAUR FACT CARDS

Euoplocephalus
(YOU-o-plo-SEFF-uh-lus)
"well-armored head"

• Larger than an automobile • 29 feet (8.8 m) long • Weighed 3 tons (2.7 metric tons) • Bony skull like a steel strong-box • Armored eyelids that clanged shut • Rows of armored spikes and knobs the length of its body • Heavy swinging tail club made of bone measured 3 feet (1 m) across • Could topple Tyrannosaurus rex • Small teeth for eating plants

Ichthyosaurus
(ICK-thee-uh-SORE-us)
"fish lizard"

• Fastest sea-going reptile • Dolphin-shaped body with fins and flippers • Breathed air • Some grew to 18 feet (5.5 m) long • Did not lay eggs • Bore live young • Very large eyes • Hunted large fish • Long mouths with many sharp tiny teeth • Ate fish and squid-like animals

Iguanadon
(ee-GWAN-uh-don)
"iguana tooth"

• Huge body stood 24 feet (7.3 m) tall and 30 feet (9.1 m) long • Traveled and ate together in herds • Stood upright on hind feet to feed on the higher leaves, or crouched low to munch low plants • 3 toes on hind feet • 3-5 fingers on short forearms and spiked thumb for gathering and eating • Thumb spike wrongly placed as a nose horn by early scientists

Mausasaurus
(MO-zuh-SORE-us)
"sea serpent"

• Large fierce aquatic lizards over 40 feet (12 m) long • Lived in an inland sea • Long powerful tail and paddle-like feet made them strong swimmers that attacked all kinds of sea animals • Long powerful jaws • Used their paddle-like legs to come ashore to sunbathe

Nodosaurus
(NOE-doe-SORE-us)
"toothless lizard"

• Completely covered with tough bony knobs and plates crossing the back in rows • Broadest at shoulder and neck • Massive spikes stuck out all along the sides • Grew to 23 feet (7 m) long • Armored skull • A bony lump with eye and nostril holes • Short sturdy legs • When attacked it dropped and gripped the ground with its sharp claws

Ornitholestes
(or-nith-uh-LESS-tees)
"bird robber"

• Small, slightly-built body was 6½ feet (2 m) long • Short deep head, powerful teeth and jaws • Working hands with 2 long fingers and opposing thumb to grasp small objects • Caught animals on the run or darted between larger carnivores to scavenge from carcasses • Agile enough to catch birds in flight • Also called *Coelurus*

Pachycephalosaurs
(PAK-ee-SEF-uh-low -SORES)
"thick-headed lizard"

• "Bone-headed" plant-eaters • Mountain goats of their time • Lived in herds or flocks • Competed to be leader by bashing heads together • Skull was a big solid lump of bone for battering • Body 6½ feet (2 m) in length • Strong back and tail vertebrae to withstand the impact • Bore live young

Parasaurolophus
(pur-uh-sore-OL-uh-fus)
"crested lizard"

• Hollow-crested duck-bill • Sweeping tubes from nostrils curved back longer than its head • 30 feet (9 m) long weighed 5 tons (4.5 metric tons) • May have made a honking or trombone-like sound as a signal, warning, or mating call • Wide flat billboard-like tail for balance or swimming

Protoceratops
(PRO-toe-SER-uh-tops)
"early horned head"

• Small barrel-shaped creature • 9 feet (2.7 m) long • Large neck frill • Short forearms • Head with sharp beak for snipping of leaves • Powerful jaw with chopping teeth • Frill not yet developed as a strong armored shield • Traveled in herds • Nests full of sausage-shaped eggs arranged in outward pointing circles

DINOSAUR FACT CARDS

Pterodactulus
(TAIR-uh-DAK-tul-us)
"winged fingers"

• The smallest pterodactyl • Pigeon-sized body • Light hollow bones • Wings to 15 feet (4.6 m) wide • Little or no tail • Leathery fur-covered skin • Large head and long nose resembling a bird's beak with sharp teeth • Probably caught insects in the air

Pteranodon
(ter-AN-uh-don)
"winged and toothless"

• Largest pterodactyl • Light-weight turkey-sized body • Wing span 25 to 50 feet (7-15 m) • Head pointed at both ends with long pointed toothless beak in front • Bony crest in back for balance • Short stumpy tail or no tail • Hung from the cliff sides head-down like a bat • Fished far out in vast shallow seas and rested on the top of waves

Quetzalcoatlas
(KET-sal-COAT-lus)

• Early short-tailed pterosaur • Largest flying creature known • Wings made of bat-like skin with a 45-foot (13.7-m) wingspan • About the size of a small airplane • Could glide long distances in the skies • Probably ate the remains of carrion (already dead carcasses)

Rhamphorhynchus
(RAM-fo-RINK-us)
"prow-beak"

• A primitive long-tailed pterosaur • Small fur-covered body • Strong leathery wings spanned a distance of 4 feet (1.2 m), supported by a long fourth finger • Long thin tail twice the length of its body ended with a rudder-like paddle • Large keen eyes • Sharp forward-slanted teeth for the gripping and eating of fish

Saltopus
(SALT-o-pus)
"leaping foot"

• A small swift meat-eater the size of a house cat • Long neck, small head, many sharp teeth • Ran upright on hind legs • 5-fingered hands enabled it to grasp small animals • Skin covered with frayed scales that some scientists believe may have developed into feathers, making them a possible bird ancestor

Stegosaurus
(STEG-uh-SORE-us)
"roof-plated lizard"

• Usually two rows of overlapping bony plates embedded in head and neck • Larger diamond-shaped plates on back and tail for protection • 2 pair of spikes on tail • 11 feet (3.4 m) high at hips, 30 feet (9 m) long • Weighed 2 tons (5.4 metric tons) • Small flat teeth for grazing on low branches and ground plants

Styracosaurus
(stu-RAK-uh-SORE-us)
"spiked lizard"

• Short neck frill opened out into six long spikes growing from rear of frill to protect its neck and frighten the enemy • Body 18 feet (5.5 m) long, 4 tons (3.6 metric tons) • Single long nose horn was main weapon • Lived in forested areas • Strong jaws ground up tough plants

Triceratops
(try-SAIR-uh-tops)
"three-horned face"

• Largest aggressive dino-rhino • 30 feet (9.1 m) long • Weighed 12 tons (10.9 metric tons) • Head a massive chunk of bone measuring 7 feet (2 m) long • Protected by three horns • 2 40-inch (1-m) horns extended from eyebrows • Nose horn short and thick • Neck frill of armored bone created war-like shield • Plant-eater, grazed near ground

Tyrannosaurus rex
(tie-RAN-uh-SORE-us REX)
"tyrant lizard king"

• Swift and deadly hunter, placid scavenger • 50 feet (15.2 m) long, 6 tons (5.4 metric tons) • Short flexible neck with huge deep skull • Enormous jaws, huge saw-edged teeth • Brain smaller than its largest tooth • Powerful hind legs, small clawed feet • Tiny arms with 2-fingered hands, probably used only to rise

EXTINCTION

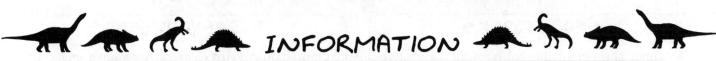

About 65 million years ago some mysterious change took place on Earth that brought a scourge of death. Scientists disagree as to what happened, but after that time almost all the dinosaurs were gone, or had become *extinct*. Scientists have proposed many theories about what might have happened, from the eating of dinosaur eggs by other animals, to massive meteorites colliding with Earth.

Many other co-existing creatures also died out, but amazingly some survived. The ammonites (shellfish) became extinct, while turtles and lobsters have changed little in 200 million years. Meat-eating sea reptiles died out, but bony ray fish and tiny land lizards were hardly affected. Sharks have been around for 400 million years. The sea crocodiles perished, but river crocodiles suffered little damage. The flying reptiles disappeared, but bird-like Archaeopteryx soared on.

PROJECT

Chart and create posters of extinction theories showing possible causes and effects.

DIRECTIONS

1. Divide class into small groups. Allow each group to choose one theory.

2. Research, discuss, and chart the possible causes and resulting effects of each theory of extinction.

3. Have each group create a poster illustrating their theory of extinction, perhaps from the dinosaurs' point of view. Glue the chart on the back of each poster.

4. Share posters with the class and put them on display.

Extended Activities:

• Hold a mock debate concerning the possible reasons for the dinosaurs' extinction.

• Propose alternative theories and find facts to support the new theory.

MATERIALS

• Resource books (See Literature List, page 3)
• Copies of Extinction Theories Cards, following
• Poster board   • Colored marking pens
• Pencils   • Rulers

EXTINCTION THEORIES

SPACE ROCKS

A comet shower or the collision of a massive meteorite would have raised dense dust clouds, spreading and blotting out heat and light. Scientists have evidence of a huge crater in the Gulf of Mexico that seems to confirm this theory. There they discovered *iridium* (often found in rocks from outer space) in layers of clay and rock dating 65 million years ago (the time of the extinction.)

EPIDEMIC DISEASE

Scientists have discovered dinosaur bones that indicate cancerous tumors in the bones. Swollen areas of tumor growth have been found in the backbones of Hadrosaurs. Just as people carry diseases into foreign lands, the ancient creatures crossing land bridges from continent to continent could have spread deadly diseases to other lands where those animals were not immune to them.

CATERPILLARS

One of the strangest theories supports the belief that hordes of caterpillars crawled across the continents eating all the plant life. Soon the plant-eating dinosaurs died off, followed by the meat-eating dinosaurs who fed on them.

POLAR WINTER

The climate change theory points out that the continents drifted away from the equator toward the polar regions. That would certainly have brought on colder weather. Extensive glacial expansion might have caused global winters over a long period of time, leaving much of the Earth frozen and barren.

EXPLODING STAR

Could extinction have been caused by an exploding star somewhere close enough in our galaxy to shower Earth with deadly radiation? It would have produced huge clouds of cosmic dust spreading through our solar system and into our atmosphere blocking our sun's heat and energy, killing off many animals and plants living on the surface.

DEADLY PLANTS

Some scientists suggest that new varieties of poisonous plants like the deadly nightshade began to flourish on Earth in the time of the mass extinction of the dinosaurs.

EGG-EATERS

One theory is that small egg-eating dinosaurs and the tiny mammals existing at that time ate all the dinosaur eggs. Among the smartest of the small dinosaurs was the Oviraptor (Oh-ve RAP-tor),"The Egg Stealer." It had to depend on its quick wit and instant reflexes to invade a Tyrannosaurus nest and and escape carrying the eggs without being caught and eaten by a distraught mother.

MOTHER NATURE

Nature often brings catastrophes that disrupt life on Earth. Could world-wide flooding have swept the dinosaurs to watery graves? Could clouds of ash from volcanic activity have killed off much of Earth's plant and animal life? Scientist know iridium also comes from the Earth's core. Is its presence in sedimentary layers a sign of a great push upwards by mountain chains that destroyed the dinosaurs?

MIX AND MATCH

INFORMATION

It is unusual for fossil hunters to find all the bones of a dinosaur laying in the original skeletal positions. More often they find a pile of many dinosaurs' bones all jumbled up together, or one creature may be scattered widely. Rebuilding the dinosaurs is a guessing game. In the beginning some paleontologists made mistakes in assembling the bones—the wrong head, a toe spike stuck on top of the head, mixed-up legs, horns or teeth. But as more and more fossil pieces are found and the information shared, the more accurate our picture becomes.

PROJECT

Create a mix-and-match dinosaur

DIRECTIONS

1. Write dinosaur names on index cards, one name per card and enough cards for each child to select three. There can be duplicate names. Put the cards in a bag.

2. Each student draws three cards (no duplicates, please!) and glues them left to right on construction paper

3. Use your knowledge about dinosaurs to create a mix-and-match dinosaur. The first card represents the dinosaur's head, the second its body, and the third its tail.

4. Reproduce and complete the Dinosaur Profile for each new and unique dinosaur.

MATERIALS

- Index cards
- Paper bag
- Marking pen
- White construction paper
- Glue
- Crayons or watercolor paints
- Dinosaur Profile, following

TRIBRONTOSTEGOSAURUS

DINOSAUR PROFILE

◎◎ NAME

What is the name of this newly discovered dinosaur? _____

◎◎ TYPE

Is this dinosaur lizard-hipped or bird-hipped? _____

◎◎ DIET

Is this dinosaur a plant or meat eater? _____

◎◎ PHYSICAL CHARACTERISTICS

Weight:

_____

Length:

_____

Height:

_____

Color:

_____

Unusual body markings, characteristics, defensive capabilities:

_____

_____

_____

Other interesting information:

_____

_____

_____

DINO GAMES

PROJECT

Play some games to reinforce your knowledge about dinosaurs.

DINO-DARE

Materials

• Fact Cards, pages 40-42
• Chalkboard or paper for scoring

Game Rules

1. Select three officials, then divide the rest of the class into teams of five or more players. Each team chooses one spokesperson.

2. The officials form a question based on information from the Fact Cards and present the challenge, "We dare you to answer this dinosaur question."

3. The question is posed to all the teams. Team members discuss the question and decide on the best answer. The spokesperson stands. The first team to stand and offer the correct response to the dare scores 3 points. A wrong choice gets a one-point deduction.

3. Continue to play for a pre-determined amount of time. The team with the most points at the end of the time is declared the winner. If there is a tie, offer one final dare.

DINO-BEE

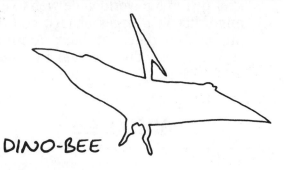

Materials

• Glossary page 4
• List of dinosaur names

Game Rules

1. Conduct a spelling bee with dinosaur names and related terms.

2. Establish spelling bee rules prior to beginning.

3. Award the winner with the title of Tyrannosaurus Speller.

DINO-TOSS

Materials

• Die
• Dinosaur names on index cards.

Game Rules

1. Challenge the whole class with this game.

2. Choose an index card. Toss the die. List a fact for the selected dinosaur to match the number shown on the die. (For example, if the number three is thrown, list three facts.)

3. Score a point for each correct fact. Select a panel of judges to rule on the correctness of each answer.

WORLD WIDE WEB.

Look in the world wide web to expand your knowledge of dinosaurs. Keep in mind that web pages change constantly. The web pages below were active at publication date but their continued presence is not guaranteed. Like an archaeologist, digging into the internet will uncover all kinds of fascinating discoveries.

ADDRESS	CONTENT
denrl.igis.uiuc.edu/isgsroot/dinos/dinos_home.html	Have you always wanted to take part in a dinosaur dig? This site includes photos from a real 1996-1997 dig and photos of ranch life during the dig.
monhome.sw2.k12.wy.us/Dinos/intro.html	Tour a dinosaur park! Articles on all kinds of dinosaurs, about who dug up bones and where, when dinosaurs lived, and more dinosaur discoveries.
www.sciencenet.org.uk/database/Archaeology/Lists/dino	ScienceNet question-and-answer website to answer questions about dinosaurs.
www.solustions.ibm.com/k12/teacher/dinoss.html	Dinosaur activities for students with a list of related websites.
kidsdinosaurs.miningco.com/msub1.htm	A list of websites and net links to help kids with dinosaur homework.